Be Filled With the Spirit

Dispelling the Myths & Revealing the Truths of Speaking in Tongues

by
David Pizzimenti

Harrison House
Tulsa, Oklahoma

Unless otherwise noted, all Scripture quotations are from the *King James Version* of the Bible.

The Scripture quotation marked AMP is taken from *The Amplified New Testament*. Copyright © 1958, 1987 by The Lockman Foundation, La Habra, California.

07 06 05 04   10 9 8 7 6 5 4 3 2 1

Be Filled With the Spirit—
Dispelling the Myths & Revealing the Truths
of Speaking in Tongues
ISBN 1-57794-605-7 (formerly ISBN 1-88008-999-8)
Copyright © 2004 by David Pizzimenti
Glory to Him Fellowship
aka David Pizzimenti Ministries
P.O. Box 1289
Ozark, Alabama 36360

Published by **Harrison House**, Inc.
P.O. Box 35035
Tulsa, Oklahoma 74153

Contents

1 Bible Answers to Eight
  Common Objections 1

2 Bible Evidence of the Infilling of
  the Holy Spirit 29

3 The Benefits of Speaking in Tongues..........57

4 Holy Spirit Manifestations 69

5 How To Be Filled With the Spirit................85

1

Bible Answers to Eight Common Objections

Very often people make not-so-scriptural objections to the scriptural experience I am about to discuss. Therefore, because I believe it is a point at which every believer can agree, I chose the following verse as my starting point:

> All Scripture is given by inspiration of God, and is profitable for doctrine, for reproof, for correction, for instruction in righteousness:
>
> that the man of God may be perfect, thoroughly furnished unto all good works.
>
> 2 Timothy 3:16,17

The Bible must be the Christian's final authority on any topic, for God inspired it.

Well-meaning Bible teachers or church traditions may have inspired our denominations, our churches, or our opinions. However, because God inspired the Bible, it should always be our final say-so in any matter.

Scripture is not designed to persuade people who have made up their minds that something it says is not for them. Rather, it is designed to bless believers who want the truth. Experience has taught me that accepting misinterpreted Scripture, or putting faith in human opinion, can create an obstacle for believers who desire everything available to them in their relationship with Jesus Christ.

For example, in Mark 16:17 Jesus said, "These signs shall follow them that believe; ...they shall speak with new tongues." One sign that follows the believer is *speaking with new tongues.* Though designated by Jesus, speaking in tongues has been debated among believers for centuries.

The following pages address eight human objections to speaking in other tongues. Some are the result of misinterpreted Scripture, while others have no biblical basis. While considering each objection, let us remember to draw our conclusions from the final authority, the Word of God, which "is given by inspiration of God, and is profitable for doctrine, for reproof, for correction, for instruction in righteousness: that the man of God may be perfect, thoroughly furnished unto all good works."

Objection One:
Speaking in Tongues Is of the Devil

Some people believe speaking in tongues is strictly of the devil. They might say, "Those people are speaking in demonic gibberish" or "They're demon possessed." However, in Scripture, Jesus makes a statement that serves to answer this objection:

> I say unto you, Ask, and it shall be given you, seek, and ye shall find; knock, and it shall be opened unto you. For every one that asketh

receiveth; and he that seeketh findeth; and to him that knocketh it shall be opened.

If a son shall ask bread of any of you that is a father, will he give him a stone? or if he ask a fish, will he for a fish give him a serpent? Or if he shall ask an egg, will he offer him a scorpion? If ye then, being evil, know how to give good gifts unto your children: how much more shall your heavenly Father give the Holy Spirit to them that ask him?

Luke 11:9-13

In this passage, Jesus says if you ask for an egg, you will not get a scorpion; if you ask for fish, you will not get a serpent; if you ask for bread, you will not get a stone. Accordingly, if you ask for the Holy Spirit, you will not get a demon.

In another account of Jesus' ministry, we find religious teachers trying to deceive Jesus' followers by saying He is acting by the power of Satan. (Mark 3.) However, Acts 10:38 says everything Jesus did was done by the power of the Holy Spirit: "...God anointed Jesus of Nazareth with the Holy Ghost and with power: who went about doing good, and healing all that were oppressed of the devil; for God was with him."

In response to the religious teachers' claims that He was acting by the power of Satan, Jesus said:

> How can Satan cast out Satan? And if a kingdom be divided against itself, that kingdom cannot stand. And if a house be divided against itself, that house cannot stand. And if Satan rise up against himself, and be divided, he cannot stand, but hath an end.
>
> Mark 3:23-26

Then Jesus issued a solemn warning:

> Verily I say unto you, All sins shall be forgiven unto the sons of men, and blasphemies wherewith soever they shall blaspheme: but he that shall blaspheme against the Holy Ghost hath never forgiveness, but is in danger of eternal damnation. Because they said, He hath an unclean spirit.
>
> Mark 3:28-30

The Holy Ghost is not an unclean spirit. He is a holy, righteous, pure Spirit; and to blaspheme

Him is to endanger oneself. According to *Webster's Dictionary* when one is guilty of blasphemy, one has insulted or shown contempt or lack of reverence for God.[1] To do so is extremely dangerous, as Hebrews 10:29-31 says:

> Of how much sorer punishment, suppose ye, shall he be thought worthy, who hath trodden under foot the Son of God, and hath counted the blood of the covenant, wherewith he was sanctified, an unholy thing, and hath done despite unto the Spirit of grace?

> For we know him that hath said, Vengeance belongeth unto me, I will recompense, saith the Lord. And again, the Lord shall judge his people. It is a fearful thing to fall into the hands of the living God.

If you believe that speaking in other tongues is not for you, then at least do not equate this experience with being demon possessed or of the devil. Whether a Christian knows better or not

---

[1] *The Merriam-Webster Dictionary*, Copyright © 1998 by Merriam-Webster, Incorporated, s.v. "blasphemy."

when making such a statement, God Almighty will be the judge.

Objection Two:
Tongues Passed Away

Many believe that tongues passed away after the Bible was completed and after the apostles' deaths. Those who believe this objection acknowledge that believers once spoke in other tongues as a sign of supernatural occurrence in the church, but that once the Scriptures were completed tongues were no longer needed.

The experience of speaking in tongues can be traced from the Day of Pentecost, through the history of those in the Middle East martyred for speaking in tongues, to the records of those in Europe and the United States finally gaining the experience. For two thousand years, speaking in tongues has been documented, and the experience has never died out. The Old Testament prophet Joel was the first to speak of the Pentecostal experience. He prophesied:

And it shall come to pass afterward, that I will pour out my spirit upon all flesh; and your sons and your daughters shall prophesy, your old men shall dream dreams, your young men shall see visions: and also upon the servants and upon the handmaids in those days will I pour out my spirit.

Joel 2:28,29

The assumption that speaking in tongues was dependent upon the length of time it took the Bible to be written has no scriptural basis. The Bible was not assembled as a book until over three hundred years after Jesus Christ was resurrected. If we believe speaking in tongues was in operation until the Bible was completed, then we also have to believe that this manifestation was in existence for at least three hundred years. This would mean God favored the believers who lived in the first three hundred years of the church over those in the last seventeen hundred years. However, the Bible says, "God is no respecter of persons" (Acts 10:34).

The assumption that speaking in tongues was dependent upon the apostles' life spans is also unsupported by Scripture. During the apostles' ministry people younger than the apostles were filled with the Holy Spirit with the evidence of speaking in other tongues. (Acts 8:14-18; 10:44-46; 19:6,7.) However, there is no Scripture to support the belief that this ability was lost after the last apostle died.

Acts 2, which records the first occurrence of people speaking in other tongues, actually answers the majority of questions on the subject. This first occurrence caused a great commotion. People were asking, "What is this? What does it mean?" Peter stood and gave this answer.

> But this is that which was spoken by the prophet Joel; and it shall come to pass in the last days, saith God, I will pour out of my Spirit upon all flesh: and your sons and your daughters shall prophesy, and your young men shall see visions, and your old men shall dream dreams.
>
> Acts 2:16,17

Peter explained that what they were hearing—people speaking in other tongues—was exactly what Joel prophesied in the Old Testament. Peter continued:

> Therefore being by the right hand of God exalted, and having received of the Father the promise of the Holy Ghost, he hath shed forth this, which ye now see and hear.
>
> Acts 2:33

The Holy Spirit cannot be seen. However, the *result* of being filled with the Holy Spirit can be seen and heard: People speak in other tongues.

> Then Peter said unto them, Repent, and be baptized every one of you in the name of Jesus Christ for the remission of sins, and ye shall receive the gift of the Holy Ghost. For the promise is unto you, and to your children, and to all that are afar off, even as many as the Lord our God shall call.
>
> Acts 2:38,39

Peter said the promise of the Holy Spirit, which had been shed forth and which his audience could see and hear, was for *all whom the Lord would call*. In other words, he said the promise of the Holy Spirit with the evidence of speaking in tongues was for *everyone who would receive Jesus as Lord and Savior*. Therefore, this promise of the Holy Spirit, which they heard and saw two thousand years ago, is still for us today. The promise never passed away.

Objection Three: Only the Apostles Could Minister the Infilling

The assumption that speaking in tongues stopped when the last apostle died carries much credence because of another false assumption. That is the idea that no one else could minister the infilling of the Holy Spirit. However, Acts 9 deflates this reasoning.

The beginning of chapter 9 records Saul on a journey to arrest Christians. Through a supernatural appearance of Jesus Christ, he is saved and told to go into Damascus, where he will be told what to do next. Saul arises and goes to the city, but for three days is blind and does not eat or drink.

Acts 9:10-12 records what happens next:

> And there was a certain disciple at Damascus, named Ananias; and to him said the Lord in a vision, Ananias. And he said, Behold, I am here, Lord.
>
> And the Lord said unto him, Arise, and go into the street which is called Straight, and enquire in the house of Judas for one called Saul, of Tarsus: for, behold, he prayeth,
>
> And hath seen in a vision a man named Ananias coming in, and putting his hand on him, that he might receive his sight.

Ananias was not one of the twelve apostles of Jesus but was "a certain *disciple*," which simply means he was a follower or student of Jesus Christ. Furthermore, he did not want to deal with Saul—and he gave the Lord his reasons. Yet the Lord encouraged and assured Ananias that Saul was His chosen vessel. As a result,

> Ananias went his way, and entered into the
> house; and putting his hands on him said,
> Brother Saul, the Lord, even Jesus, that
> appeared unto thee in the way as thou camest,
> hath sent me, that thou mightest receive thy
> sight, and be filled with the Holy Ghost.
>
> Acts 9:17

In this context, we can understand Paul's gratitude for the ability to speak in tongues, as stated in 1 Corinthians 14:18: "I thank my God, I speak with tongues more than ye all." This champion tongue talker of the New Testament was ministered the infilling of the Holy Spirit not by an apostle but by a "certain disciple," Ananias, who could just as easily have been you or I. This disproves the objection that only the apostles could minister the infilling of the Holy Spirit.

Objection Four:
Tongues Are Not for Everyone

Some believe that tongues are not for everyone but for only a select few. One Scripture generally used to support this objection is 1 Corinthians 12:30, which says, "Have all the gifts of healing? do all speak with tongues? do all interpret?" Obviously, the answer to each question is no, and people interpret this to mean that not every believer can receive the gift of speaking in tongues.

However, the topic in 1 Corinthians 12 is not that of being filled with the Holy Spirit but rather the nine gifts of the Spirit, which are public ministry manifestations. Only two of the nine gifts of the Spirit are unique to the New Testament; the other seven existed in the Old Testament. All nine gifts, which are in manifestation in the Church Age, are taught in this chapter.

Starting in verse 8, the nine gifts (public ministry manifestations) are discussed: the word of wisdom, the word of knowledge, discerning of spirits, and so forth. Not everyone is in public ministry, but in public ministry the Spirit divides the gifts as He wills. The surrounding verses show us the context of this matter:

God hath set some in the church, first apostles, secondarily prophets, thirdly teachers, after that miracles, then gifts of healings, helps, governments, diversities of tongues.

Are all apostles? are all prophets? are all teachers? are all workers of miracles? Have all the gifts of healing? do all speak with tongues? do all interpret? But covet earnestly the best gifts....

1 Corinthians 12:28-31

In order to understand the Scriptures, we must determine the following: (1) whether a verse is speaking literally or allegorically, (2) the context of the verse, and (3) what other Scriptures have to say about the same subject.

In view of these rules, 1 Corinthians 12:30 does not prove that being filled with the Holy Spirit with the evidence of speaking in tongues is not for everyone. Rather, it states that, just as not every believer is called and equipped to be an apostle or prophet or teacher, not every believer is equipped to publicly minister in tongues or to interpret tongues given in public services.

Objection Five:
Tongues Shall Cease

Some people believe that tongues have ceased. This objection to speaking in tongues in this present age is based in part on a misinterpretation of 1 Corinthians 13:8, which says:

> Charity never faileth: but whether there be prophecies, they shall fail; whether there be tongues, they shall cease; whether there be knowledge, it shall vanish away.

Verse 10 states when tongues shall cease:

> But when that which is perfect is come, then that which is in part shall be done away.

Some people think that *which is perfect* refers to the Word of God, so they believe that upon completion of the Bible's writing tongues were no longer needed. However, the context of the passage discredits this theory. Verses 11-12 say:

> When I was a child, I spake as a child, I understood as a child, I thought as a child: but when I became a man, I put away childish

things. For now we see through a glass, darkly; but then face to face: now I know in part; but then shall I know even as also I am known.

"That which is perfect" will come when the "face to face" time comes: when we see Jesus face to face. Then we will know everything; all our questions will be answered; we will know ourselves as God knows us. When this time of "that which is perfect" comes, we will have no need for tongues.

Furthermore, this passage shows us that if we believe tongues ceased when the Bible was written, we must also believe knowledge ceased when the Bible was written. Both are in the same verse: "...whether there be tongues, they shall cease; whether there be knowledge, it shall vanish away."

Knowledge certainly has not vanished. In fact, Daniel 12:4 says in the end "knowledge shall be increased." Knowledge will increase and not vanish in the last days, and the same will be true of speaking in other tongues—until "that which is perfect" has come. The objection that tongues ceased when the Bible was completed cannot be substantiated in light of the full context of the Scriptures.

Objection Six:
Salvation and Baptism of
the Holy Spirit Are One

Some people maintain that we receive the baptism of the Holy Spirit when we are saved. They contend that there is not a separate experience and that we receive all of the Holy Spirit when we accept Jesus as Lord and Savior. Contrarily, the Bible indicates an experience with the Holy Spirit subsequent to and distinct from salvation.

For example, note Jesus' instructions for His disciples regarding the Holy Spirit. John tells us Jesus breathed on the disciples after His resurrection: "And when he had said this, he breathed on them, and saith unto them, Receive ye the Holy Ghost" (John 20:22). In full context, we can see that they received the Holy Spirit, were born again, and became new creatures at that moment.

Later, though, in the first chapter of Acts, He commanded the apostles to "wait for the promise of the Father," which He called a baptism in the Holy Ghost.

> And, being assembled together with them, commanded them that they should not depart from Jerusalem, but wait for *the promise of the Father,* which, saith he, ye have heard of me. For John truly baptized with water, but ye shall be *baptized with the Holy Ghost* not many days hence.
>
> Acts 1:4,5

Jesus was telling these same apostles to whom He had said, "Receive the Holy Spirit," not to leave until they were baptized with the Holy Spirit. He was indicating a subsequent, distinct experience from the salvation experience. Then, in verse 8 He says:

> But ye shall receive power, after that the Holy Ghost is come upon you: and ye shall be

witnesses unto me both in Jerusalem, and in all Judaea, and in Samaria, and unto the uttermost part of the earth.

The Holy Spirit is not two people. However, He does have more than one function. We receive the indwelling presence of the Holy Spirit when we are saved; however, the *indwelling presence* of the Holy Spirit is not synonymous with the *infilling* of the Holy Spirit, which is signified by speaking in other tongues. The *infilling* of the Holy Spirit is exactly what happened to the believers who obeyed Jesus' command and tarried in Jerusalem to receive the power of the Holy Spirit.

And when the day of Pentecost was fully come, they were all with one accord in one place. And suddenly there came a sound from heaven as of a rushing mighty wind, and it filled all the house where they were sitting. And there appeared unto them cloven tongues like as of fire, and it sat upon each of them. And they were all filled with the Holy Ghost,

and began to speak with other tongues, as the
Spirit gave them utterance.

Acts 2:1-4

If these individuals had already received *all*
that was available to them, Jesus would not have
instructed them to wait for the promise of the
Holy Spirit.

Later on, in Paul's travels to Ephesus, Paul
asks some disciples, "Have ye received the Holy
Ghost since ye believed?" If these individuals
had received the entire ministry of the Holy
Spirit when they believed, Paul would not have
asked the question. There was obviously something more.

Earlier, Jesus referred to the infilling of the
Holy Spirit:

In the last day, that great day of the feast,
Jesus stood and cried, saying, If any man thirst,
let him come unto me, and drink. He that
believeth on me, as the Scripture hath said, out
of his belly shall flow rivers of living water.

John 7:37,38

The distinction between the *indwelling* presence of the Holy Spirit received at the moment of salvation and the *infilling* of the Holy Spirit (also called the *baptism of the Holy Spirit*) accompanied by speaking in other tongues, is supported by these and numerous other Scriptures.

Objection Seven:
Spirit-filled With No Evidence
of Speaking in Tongues

Some believers argue, "I know I'm filled with the Holy Spirit, and I don't speak in other tongues." However, in the five biblical accounts of the infilling of the Holy Spirit, the evidence was the believers' ability to speak in other tongues. Look, for example, at the three following passages:

> And they were all filled with the Holy Ghost, and began to speak with other tongues, as the Spirit gave them utterance.
>
> Acts 2:4

While Peter yet spake these words, the Holy Ghost fell on all them which heard the word. And they of the circumcision which believed were astonished, as many as came with Peter, because that on the Gentiles also was poured out the gift of the Holy Ghost. For they heard them speak with tongues, and magnify God. Then answered Peter, Can any man forbid water, that these should not be baptized, which have received the Holy Ghost as well as we?

Acts 10:44-47

And when Paul had laid his hands upon them, the Holy Ghost came on them; and they spake with tongues, and prophesied.

Acts 19:6

In a fourth passage, in which Peter and John pray for Philip's Samaritan converts (Acts 8:14-24), there is no mention of tongues. However, Simon the sorcerer "saw that through laying on of the apostles' hands the Holy Ghost was given" (v. 18). Paul says in 1 Corinthians 14:22 that tongues are a sign to unbelievers. For Simon to have *seen* that the Holy Spirit was given, there must have been a sign: something visible and/or audible in the physical realm.

Finally, Paul's baptism of the Holy Spirit, the fifth example in Scripture, does not show him speaking in tongues when Ananias ministers to him (Acts 9). However, in 1 Corinthians 14:18 he gives testimony to the fact that "I speak with tongues more than ye all." In fact, he makes this statement within the most powerful teaching in Scripture regarding God's will for tongues in the church.

Tongues have always been the *initial evidence* of receiving the infilling, or baptism, of the Holy Spirit. Paul teaches us in 2 Corinthians 13:1, "In the mouth of two or three witnesses shall every word be established." On the issue of tongues, the Bible did not give two or three witnesses, but five!

Objection Eight:
Jesus Didn't Speak in Tongues

Some people rationalize that since Jesus didn't speak in other tongues, we do not need to. However, the reason Jesus did not speak in other tongues was that He ministered under the old covenant. Tongues and interpretation of tongues did not exist until after His ascension. Speaking in tongues occurred for the first time on the Day of Pentecost:

> And when the day of Pentecost was fully come, they were all with one accord in one place. And suddenly there came a sound from heaven as of a rushing mighty wind, and it filled all the house where they were sitting. And there appeared unto them cloven tongues like as of fire, and it sat upon each of them. And they were all filled with the Holy Ghost, and began to speak with other tongues, as the Spirit gave them utterance.
>
> Acts 2:1-4

Jesus ministered under the old covenant, in which the baptism of the Holy Spirit was not available. The Holy Spirit, the Comforter, had not been given, nor could He be given until Jesus paid the price for sin on the cross, was resurrected, and ascended to the Father.

Seven gifts were in operation in the Old Testament, but on the Day of Pentecost tongues and the interpretation of tongues were added. These two additional gifts are the supernatural mark of the Church Age (Mark 16:17), a sign to the unbeliever (1 Cor. 14:22), a gift to edify the church (1 Cor. 14:4,5), and an agent to intercede before our heavenly Father (Rom. 8:26).

The New Testament brought with it tongues and the interpretation of tongues. By the time the baptism of the Holy Spirit came and tongues were manifested, Jesus was with the Father in heaven. He had done everything necessary to save us and give us both the *indwelling presence* and *infilling power* of the Holy Spirit.

The Reality of the Infilling

I trust the answers to these eight common objections to the infilling of the Holy Spirit with the evidence of speaking in tongues will be a helpful resource for you. By the time you complete this study, there should be no doubt in your mind of the reality of the infilling of the Holy Spirit, and that it is subsequent to and separate from salvation. As a result, you will be able to share these rich scriptural truths with others.

2

Bible Evidence of the Infilling of the Holy Spirit

Scripture from the Old Testament to the New makes reference to the infilling of the Holy Spirit. In Scripture, water, wine, oil, and fire are all types of the Holy Spirit. In the gospel of John as Jesus ministers to the woman at the well, He introduces the comparison between water and the Holy Spirit.

> Jesus answered and said unto her, Whosoever drinketh of this water shall thirst again: but whosoever drinketh of the water that I shall give him shall never thirst; but the water that I shall give him shall be in him a well of water springing up into everlasting life.
>
> John 4:13,14

Jesus is talking about water coming from a well. Isaiah 12:3 says, "Therefore with joy shall ye draw water out of the wells of salvation." Jesus is telling the woman that once she drinks of the well of salvation she will never thirst again; eternal life will be imparted into her spirit.

Later on in the gospel of John, Jesus describes the Holy Spirit as *rivers of living water.*

> In the last day, that great day of the feast, Jesus stood and cried, saying, If any man thirst, let him come unto me, and drink. He that believeth on me, as the Scripture hath said, out of his belly shall flow *rivers of living water.* (But this spake he of the Spirit, which they that believe on him should receive: for the Holy Ghost was not yet given; because that Jesus was not yet glorified.)
>
> John 7:37-39

A well of water is vastly different from a flowing river. Life is drawn from a well for the nourishment of the body, but a river releases power. The rivers of living water of which Jesus spoke in John 7 are a spiritual power that can flow from every believer.

Receive the Holy Spirit

John 7:39 says, "The Holy Ghost was not yet given; because that Jesus was not yet glorified." Then in John 20, as the resurrected Jesus meets with His disciples, we see the results of His being glorified.

> Then said Jesus to them again, Peace be unto you: as my Father hath sent me, even so send I you. And when he had said this, he breathed on them, and saith unto them, Receive ye the Holy Ghost.
>
> John 20:21,22

When Jesus breathed on them and said, "Receive ye the Holy Ghost," they received the Holy Spirit. This bears noticeable resemblance to the creation of man as recorded in the book of Genesis.

> And the Lord God formed man of the dust of the ground, and breathed into his nostrils the breath of life; and man became a living soul.
>
> Genesis 2:7

In the very beginning, when God created man, He breathed into him the breath of life— "and man became a living soul." Similarly, after being glorified, Jesus breathed into man the Holy Spirit—and his spirit became alive. Each one received the *indwelling presence* of the Holy Spirit; each one became born again, a new creation in Christ Jesus. (2 Cor. 5:17.)

Mark 16:15-16 records what happened next. Having just breathed on them and said, "Receive ye the Holy Ghost," Jesus continues:

> Go ye into all the world, and preach the gospel to every creature. He that believeth and is baptized shall be saved; but he that believeth not shall be damned. And these signs shall follow them that believe; in my name shall they cast out devils; they shall speak with new tongues.
>
> Mark 16:15-17

Jesus suddenly switched the subject from salvation to signs that would characterize the believing ones. These were separate and distinct subjects. He told these born-again believers, these people on whom He breathed, that now they were commissioned to go and take this message and share it, and that everyone who believed and was baptized would be saved. Once they were saved, five signs would follow the believing ones. One of the five signs was that they would speak with other tongues.

Luke, an apostle and the author of the book of Acts, documented some events of Jesus that are very important for us to understand. Acts 1:4-5 records the moments before Jesus' departure from earth, after which He would be at the right hand of the Father until His return.

> And, being assembled together with them, commanded them that they should not depart from Jerusalem, but wait for the promise of the Father, which, saith he, ye have heard of me. For John truly baptized with water; but ye shall

be baptized with the Holy Ghost not many days hence.

Acts 1:4,5

Now, as you look at verse 8, you will notice what seems to be a slightly different perspective.

> But ye shall receive power, after that the Holy Ghost is come upon you: and ye shall be witnesses unto me both in Jerusalem, and in all Judaea, and in Samaria, and unto the uttermost part of the earth.

John 20 established that these people were born again because Jesus breathed on them and said, "Receive ye the Holy Ghost." Then, in Acts 1:8, He says, "Ye shall receive power, after that the Holy Spirit is come upon you." At first glance, it may seem that Jesus was confused. In one instance, the Holy Spirit is received, and later Jesus says they will receive power after the Holy Spirit has come upon them.

However, Jesus was not confused. He was speaking of two distinct experiences. The Spirit comes *in* you when you are born again, but in Acts 1:8 Jesus was talking about the Spirit coming *upon* you. In verse 4 He talked about the "promise of the Father." He mentioned that they heard this about Him from John the Baptist. When John was baptizing with water, he said, "I indeed baptize you with water; but one mightier than I cometh, the latchet of whose shoes I am not worthy to unloose: he shall baptize you with the Holy Ghost and with fire" (Luke 3:16).

In four out of four gospels, John the Baptist says that Jesus would baptize us in the Holy Spirit. (Matt. 3:11; Mark 1:8; Luke 3:16; John 1:33.) This is a message from heaven that God wanted us to receive!

In Acts 1:4 Jesus *commanded* (not requested) His followers to wait for the promise of the Father, which was the promise of the Holy Spirit. In Mark 16 Jesus had told the disciples, "Go ye into all the world, and preach the gospel to every creature. He that believeth and is baptized shall be saved" (vv. 15,16). They must have immediately started preaching because by the time of Acts 1:15, their number had grown to 120. On the Day of Pentecost, these 120 born-again Christians (among whom were the apostles and Jesus' mother, Mary) gathered to wait, as Jesus had commanded.

> And when the day of Pentecost was fully come, they were all with one accord in one place. And suddenly there came a sound from heaven as of a rushing mighty wind, and it filled all the house where they were sitting. And there appeared unto them cloven tongues like as of fire, and it sat upon each of them. And they were all filled with the Holy Ghost, and began to speak with other tongues, as the Spirit gave them utterance.
>
> Acts 2:1-4

These 120 people had been born again and therefore had received the Holy Spirit, but on the Day of Pentecost they received an additional experience with the Holy Spirit: They were "filled with the Holy Ghost, and began to speak with other tongues, as the Spirit gave them utterance."

They went out from the Upper Room staggering under the power of God. The Bible actually says that those who saw them thought they were drunk. Religious people from all over the world were gathered in Jerusalem for the Feast of Pentecost,

> And they were all amazed, and were in doubt, saying to one another, What meaneth this? Others mocking said, These men are full of new wine.
>
> Acts 2:12,13

Two thousand years later people are as amazed, doubting, and mocking of this experience as the spectators in Acts were. However, Peter set the precedent for us who believe when he got up and said:

> For these are not drunken, as ye suppose, seeing it is but the third hour of the day. But this is that which was spoken by the prophet Joel; and it shall come to pass in the last days,

saith God, I will pour out of my Spirit upon all flesh: and your sons and your daughters shall prophesy, and your young men shall see visions, and your old men shall dream dreams: and on my servants and on my handmaidens I will pour out in those days of my Spirit; and they shall prophesy.

Acts 2:15-18

After quoting Joel and later King David, Peter said:

> Therefore being by the right of hand of God exalted, and having received of the Father the promise of the Holy Ghost, he hath shed forth this, which you now see and hear.

Acts 2:33

Peter said what the crowds saw and heard was the promise of the Holy Spirit which Jesus spoke about when He said, "Behold, I send the promise of my Father upon you: but tarry ye in the city of Jerusalem, until ye be endued with power from on high" (Luke 24:49). Jesus called this enduing "the promise of my Father." On the

Day of Pentecost, as the multitude heard and saw, they were convinced this was of God and they wanted to know how to be saved.

Recall that Jesus said, "He that believeth and is baptized shall be saved" (Mark 16:16). Now in Acts, Peter says, "Repent, and be baptized every one of you in the name of Jesus Christ for the remission of sins..." (Acts 2:38). However, Jesus didn't stop with salvation, and neither did Peter. Jesus said, "And these signs shall follow them that believe; ...they shall speak with new tongues" (Mark 16:17). Accordingly, Peter said,

> ...and ye shall receive the gift of the Holy Ghost. For the promise is unto you, and to your children, and to all that are afar off, even as many as the Lord our God shall call.
>
> Acts 2:38,39

The gift of the Holy Spirit and the promise of the Holy Spirit refer to the infilling of the Holy Spirit with the evidence of speaking in tongues. "The promise" was revealed in Acts 1:4 when

Jesus said to "wait for the promise of the Father." This gift, this promise, was seen and heard by witnesses on the Day of Pentecost, as Acts 2:1-4 reveals.

First, a *sound* was heard from heaven as "of a rushing mighty wind." Second, fire appeared as "cloven tongues like as of fire." Literally, this fire was light. The light of God shone on them. (In the Old and New Testaments bright shining light was oftentimes referred to as fire.) Third, they were *heard* speaking in tongues. Fourth, they acted like drunk people: "These men are full of new wine" (v. 13).

Five Recorded Instances in Acts of the Holy Spirit Baptism

This infilling of "new wine," as Peter called it, is a prominent topic in the book of Acts. In fact, the book of Acts contains five clear records of believers receiving the baptism of the Holy Spirit.

FIRST OCCURRENCE

Acts 2:4, which we have studied in this chapter, records the first occurrence of the outpouring of the Holy Spirit: the Day of Pentecost.

SECOND OCCURRENCE

Acts 8 documents the second instance of believers receiving the baptism of the Holy Spirit, which took place some eight years after the first.

> Then Philip went down to the city of Samaria, and preached Christ unto them. And the people with one accord gave heed unto those things which Philip spake, hearing and seeing the miracles which he did. For unclean spirits, crying with loud voice, came out of many that were possessed with them: and many taken with palsies, and that were lame, were healed. And there was great joy in that city.
>
> But when they believed Philip preaching the things concerning the kingdom of God, and the name of Jesus Christ, they were baptized, both men and women.
>
> Acts 8:5-8,12

This passage says that the people (1) gave heed to what he was saying, (2) believed the things that he preached about the Kingdom, (3) believed in Jesus, and (4) were baptized. In Mark 16 Jesus said those who believe and are baptized shall be saved. Therefore, when the people believed Philip's preaching about the kingdom of God and the name of Jesus and were baptized, they were saved and received the indwelling presence of the Holy Spirit.

> Now when the apostles which were at Jerusalem heard that Samaria had received the word of God, they sent unto them Peter and John: who, when they were come down, prayed for them, that they might receive the Holy Ghost: (for as yet he was fallen upon none of them: only they were baptized in the name of the Lord Jesus.)
>
> Acts 8:14-16

When the apostles in Jerusalem heard about these new Samaritan believers who had not yet experienced the subsequent infilling of the Holy Spirit, they sent in the two "specialists," Peter

42

and John. Acts 8:17-21 records what happened when Peter and John arrived:

> Then laid they their hands on them, and they received the Holy Ghost.
>
> And *when Simon saw* that through laying on of the apostles' hands the Holy Ghost was given, he offered them money, saying, Give me also this power, that on whomsoever I lay hands, he may receive the Holy Ghost.
>
> But Peter said unto him, Thy money perish with thee, because thou hast thought that the gift of God may be purchased with money. Thou hast neither part nor lot in this matter, for thy heart is not right in the sight of God.

Simon the sorcerer saw the manifestations of the infilling of the Holy Spirit—he saw and heard them doing something—and he was willing to pay money for the ability to bestow this experience on others. However, Peter said he couldn't buy it because the promise of the Father is the gift of the Holy Spirit. This gift is given to those whose hearts are right in the sight of God, and obviously Simon's heart was not right.

Note the similarities in the experience and the manifestations in Acts 2:4 and Acts 8:17-21. Both record an audible and visible result of the infilling of the Holy Spirit.

Third Occurrence

The third recorded occurrence of the infilling of the Holy Spirit is Saul's experience, found in Acts 9.

> And as he journeyed, he came near Damascus: and suddenly there shined round about him a light from heaven: and he fell to the earth, and heard a voice saying unto him, Saul, Saul, why persecutest thou me? And he said, Who art thou, Lord? And the Lord said, I am Jesus whom thou persecutest.... And he trembling and astonished said, Lord, what wilt thou have me to do? And the Lord said unto him, Arise, and go into the city, and it shall be told thee what thou must do.... And there was a certain disciple at Damascus, named Ananias; and to him said the Lord in a vision, Ananias. And he said, Behold, I am here, Lord. And the Lord said unto him, Arise, and...

enquire in the house of Judas for one called Saul.... Then Ananias answered, Lord, I have heard by many of this man, how much evil he hath done to thy saints at Jerusalem: and here he hath authority from the chief priests to bind all that call on thy name. But the Lord said unto him, Go thy way: for he is a chosen vessel unto me....

And Ananias went his way, and entered into the house; and putting his hands on him said, Brother Saul, the Lord, even Jesus, that appeared unto thee in the way as thou camest, hath sent me, that thou mightest receive thy sight, and be filled with the Holy Ghost.

Acts 9:3-6,10,11,13-15,17

Previously, Saul was breathing threats and slaughter against the disciples. (v. 1.) However, right there on the road to Damascus Saul was changed. Three witnesses from the Word of God indicate that Saul was born again during this time:

(1) Saul called Jesus "Lord" and did what Jesus told him to do. (v. 6,8.)

(2) Jesus called Saul a "chosen vessel." (v. 15.)

(3) Ananias called Saul "brother." (v. 17.)

Therefore, we see evidence that Saul is born again, and subsequently Ananias prays for him not only to have his vision restored but also to be filled with the Holy Spirit. The result is instantaneous.

> And immediately there fell from his eyes as it had been scales: and he received sight forthwith, and arose, and was baptized.
>
> Acts 9:18

Not only did Paul receive his healing with the evidence of his sight, but he was filled with the Holy Spirit with the evidence of speaking in tongues. Later in 1 Corinthians 14:15 Paul writes, "I will pray with the spirit, and I will pray with the understanding also: I will sing with the spirit, and I will sing with the understanding also." Then in 1 Corinthians 14:18 Paul writes, "I thank my God, I speak with tongues more than ye all."

We know for a fact from Scripture that the entire New Testament, with the possible exception of one or two books, was written by people who were filled with the Holy Spirit with the evidence of speaking in tongues. As the recipient of the third recorded occurrence of the infilling of the Holy Spirit, Paul alone wrote two-thirds of the New Testament.

Fourth Occurrence

Acts 10 is the fourth recorded occurrence of the infilling of the Holy Spirit, and it happened ten years after the Day of Pentecost. Recall that every time there was such an experience subsequent to salvation, the evidence manifested is speaking in tongues. Now in Acts 10, as Peter preaches in the house of Cornelius the centurion, the same is about to happen:

> How God anointed Jesus of Nazareth with the Holy Ghost and with power: who went about doing good, and healing all that were oppressed of the devil; for God was with him. And we are witnesses of all things which he did both in the land of the Jews, and in Jerusalem; whom they slew and hanged on a tree: Him

God raised up the third day, and shewed him openly; not to all the people, but unto witnesses chosen before God, even to us, who did eat and drink with him after he rose from the dead. And he commanded us to preach unto the people, and to testify that it is he which was ordained of God to be the Judge of quick and dead. To him give all the prophets witness, that through his name whosoever believeth in him shall receive remission of sins.

Acts 10:38-43

Peter preached the salvation message of the Gospel, and evidently the people listening believed and became saved because "while Peter yet spake these words, the Holy Ghost fell on all them which heard the word" (v. 44). Verses 45-48 tell us what happened next:

They of the circumcision which believed were astonished, as many as came with Peter, because that on the Gentiles also was poured out the gift of the Holy Ghost. For they heard them speak with tongues, and magnify God.

Then answered Peter, Can any man forbid water, that these should not be baptized, which have received the Holy Ghost as well as we? And he commanded them to be baptized in the name of the Lord. Then prayed they him to tarry certain days.

Acts 10:45-48

Peter preached the Gospel, in which Jesus said *whosoever* will believe and is baptized will be saved. He knew they had accepted Jesus as Savior because, as verse 46 says, he "heard them speak with tongues."

Not only were these Gentiles saved, but they were filled with Holy Spirit! In fact, Peter said they received the same gift he had received! So Peter asked the witnesses, "Can any man forbid water, that these should not be baptized, which have received the Holy Ghost as well as we?" What convinced the witnesses was that "they heard them speak with tongues, and magnify God" (v. 46). That was the evidence!

Then when Peter and the brethren went back to Jerusalem, they were questioned by the Jerusalem church brethren, "What were you doing down there with those Gentiles, those unclean people?" they asked. So Peter started telling them about the vision and the voice that told him to go and fear no man. Giving his defense, the apostle related how he brought witnesses with him and went to the Gentiles.

And the Spirit bade me go with them, nothing doubting. Moreover these six brethren accompanied me, and we entered into the man's house: and he shewed us how he had seen an angel in his house, which stood and said unto him, Send men to Joppa, and call for Simon, whose surname is Peter; who shall tell thee words, whereby thou and all thy house shall be saved.

And as I began to speak, the Holy Ghost fell on them, as on us at the beginning. Then remembered I the word of the Lord, how that he said, John indeed baptized with water; but ye shall be baptized with the Holy Ghost. Forasmuch then as God gave them the like gift as he did unto us, who believed on the Lord Jesus Christ; what was I, that I could withstand God?

> When they heard these things, they held
> their peace, and glorified God, saying, Then
> hath God also to the Gentiles granted repen-
> tance unto life.
>
> Acts 11:12-18

Peter knew the Gentiles received the same gift
that he had received ten years earlier because he
heard the Gentiles speak in tongues. It was this
very evidence which convinced Peter that these
people were genuinely saved. He used it in his
defense when he said, "What was I, that I could
withstand God?"

Then, these members of the church in
Jerusalem said, "Then hath God also to the
Gentiles granted repentance unto life." The evi-
dence that convinced the apostles was the
Gentiles' ability to speak in other tongues.

FIFTH OCCURRENCE

The fifth recorded occurrence of the infilling
of the Holy Spirit is found in Acts 19. Ten years
had passed since Peter was at Cornelius's house.

It was approximately twenty years after the Day of Pentecost, and Paul was ministering in Ephesus.

> And it came to pass, that, while Apollos was at Corinth, Paul having passed through the upper coasts came to Ephesus: and finding certain disciples, he said unto them, Have ye received the Holy Ghost since ye believed? And they said unto him, We have not so much as heard whether there be any Holy Ghost. And he said unto them, Unto what then were ye baptized? And they said, Unto John's baptism. Then said Paul, John verily baptized with the baptism of repentance, saying unto the people, that they should believe on him which should come after him, that is, on Christ Jesus. When they heard this, they were baptized in the name of the Lord Jesus.
>
> Acts 19:1-5

In Mark 16:16 Jesus said, "He that believeth and is baptized shall be saved." These certain disciples were not saved when Paul met them; they had only received John's baptism of repentance. They became saved after Paul told them of Jesus Christ. (v. 5.) Then, according to verse 6, "when Paul had laid his hands upon them, the Holy Ghost came on them; and they spake with tongues, and prophesied."

They had an experience with the Holy Spirit subsequent to and distinct from salvation: the indwelling power of the Holy Spirit.

A Subsequent and Distinct Experience

If we receive all there is of the ministry of the Holy Spirit at the moment of salvation, then the disciples would have spoken in tongues when Jesus breathed on them and said, "Receive ye the Holy Ghost" (John 20:22). BORN AGAIN

Similarly, the believers in Samaria would have spoken in tongues as soon as they believed and were baptized in the name of Jesus when Philip preached to them in Acts 8:12. They wouldn't have needed the other disciples to minister to them. (Acts 8:14-17.) Therefore, the infilling of the Holy Spirit is a subsequent and distinct experience.

When Paul asked the Ephesian disciples, "Have ye received the Holy Ghost since ye believed?" he implied that we don't receive all there is concerning the Holy Spirit at the moment of salvation. Of course this does not mean we can't be born again and filled with the Holy Spirit simultaneously, as Cornelius and his household were.

Notice how the manifestation of the Holy Spirit remains constant. Acts 19:6 says, "And when Paul had laid his hands upon them, the Holy Ghost came on them; and they spake with tongues, and prophesied."

Five out of five times when people were filled with the Holy Spirit, there were manifestations: sounds, fires, and prophecies. They magnified God, praised Him, and spoke in tongues. Only one of these manifestations was uniquely present on each occasion. The sign was the evidence of speaking in other tongues. Five times in the Bible believers received the Holy Spirit, and five times they spoke with other tongues.

Sometimes there were other signs involved, but the evidence of speaking in other tongues was the consistent indication that believers were filled with the Holy Spirit.

3

The Benefits of Speaking in Tongues

Jesus desires—and even commanded (Acts 1:4)—that each of His followers receive the Holy Spirit. The benefits of this experience are many. In Acts 1:8, for example, Jesus said that we would be endued with power from on high when we are baptized with the Holy Spirit.

Paul also expressed his desire that every believer would speak in tongues:

> I would that ye all spake with tongues....
> Wherefore, brethren, covet to prophesy, and forbid not to speak with tongues. Let all things be done decently and in order.
>
> 1 Corinthians 14:5,39,40

According to Paul, every believer should be able to partake of this powerful blessing of the Spirit-filled life. The starting point, of course, is to be filled with the Holy Spirit with the evidence of speaking in tongues. From there, we should be in a state of *being filled* to overflowing with the presence of God. (Eph. 5:18.)

Because we have been *filled* once doesn't mean we are *filled* today in the true sense of the word. Ephesians talks of *constantly being filled to overflowing.* Certainly, if we are filled with the Spirit, we have the Person of the Holy Spirit in our lives, but it is important to yield every day to allow Him to express Himself in our lives. We do just that by spending time daily praying in other tongues.

When we take the time to pray in tongues, we will see many benefits in our lives. Let's look at some of the benefits that God's Word has promised.

Personal and Public Edification

First Corinthians 14:4 says, "He that speaketh in an unknown tongue edifies himself...." *W. E. Vine's Expository Dictionary* relates this experience to *building ourselves up.*[2] The analogy is putting jumper cables on a low battery and charging it back up. Speaking in tongues will edify and build up our spirit.

Jude 20-21 tells us, "But ye, beloved, building up yourselves on your most holy faith, praying in the Holy Ghost, keep yourselves in the love of God, looking for the mercy of our Lord Jesus Christ unto eternal life." The ability to speak in tongues is a tool to help build us up for every-day living. It strengthens us to rise above *all* things that try to come against us.

Romans 12:2 tells us, "Be ye transformed by the renewing of your mind." We renew our mind through studying the Scriptures, while we

---

[2] *W.E. Vine, An Expository Dictionary of New Testament Words* (Old Tappan, New Jersey: Fleming H. Revell Company, 1966), pp. 17-18, S.V. "EDIFICATION, EDIFY, EDIFYING."

build up our spirit by conversing with God through the Holy Spirit. We apply a good principle (praying in the Holy Spirit) and get good results (edification, for example) because the Bible says it is so—not necessarily because we know how or why it works.

First Corinthians 14:14 in *The Amplified Bible* says:

> For if I pray in an [unknown] tongue, my spirit [by the Holy Spirit within me] prays, but my mind is unproductive [it bears no fruit and helps nobody].

Then in verse 15 Paul concludes, "What is it then? [What am I going to do?] I will pray with the spirit, and I will pray with the understanding also: I will sing with the spirit, and I will sing with the understanding also." He would pray and sing to God in the spirit (by the Holy Spirit within him) and in truth (with his intelligence and his understanding) in order to edify not only himself, but also unbelievers and the church.

Furthermore, he encouraged us to edify the church with the gifts of the Spirit, including tongues and interpretation:

> How is it then, brethren? when ye come together, every one of you hath a psalm, hath a doctrine, hath a tongue, hath a revelation, hath an interpretation. Let all things be done unto edifying.
>
> 1 Corinthians 14:26

Giving Thanks Well

In 1 Corinthians 14:16-17, Paul tells us another benefit of praying in tongues:

> Else when thou shalt bless with the spirit, how shall he that occupieth the room of the unlearned say Amen at thy giving of thanks, seeing he understandeth not what thou sayest? For thou verily givest thanks well, but the other is not edified.

When we speak in tongues, without an interpretation, our minds do not comprehend the words. However, Paul says that we give thanks well when we speak in tongues. We could simply be thanking God for being our Father or for having imparted eternal life into our spirit. We may not know, but our Father knows and loves to hear His children say, "Thank You."

Assurance and Relationship

In John 14:16-18, Jesus tells us another benefit of the infilling of the Holy Spirit:

> And I will pray the Father, and he shall give you another Comforter, that he may abide with you for ever, even the Spirit of truth; whom the world cannot receive, because it seeth him not, neither knoweth him: but ye know him; for he dwelleth with you, and shall be in you. I will not leave you comfortless: I will come to you.

We can embrace this passage of Scripture, accept it in faith, and bask in the truth of it: The Holy Spirit, the Comforter, is with us. Jesus said that He would never leave us or forsake us but would send us another Comforter. He would come to us in the Person of the Holy Spirit and never leave us comfortless. The world cannot receive Him and doesn't even know Him, but we know Him. He is with us, and He is in us. He will abide with us forever.

We can hold on to these verses and enjoy them, but there is something about praying in the Holy Spirit that makes these promises even more real. When we speak in tongues we are assured of the truth of the presence of the Holy Spirit in our lives. We are also reminded of our relationship with the Father in the presence of the Comforter, who is here to help us by showing us the way back to God. He is here to point us to the blood of Jesus Christ, to confession and repentance of sin, and to a victorious, overcoming life.

Rest and Refreshing

God promised through the prophet Isaiah that speaking in tongues also brings rest and refreshing.

> For precept must be upon precept, precept upon precept; line upon line, line upon line; here a little, and there a little: for

with stammering lips and another tongue
will he speak to this people. To whom he
said, This is the rest wherewith ye may cause
the weary to rest; and this is the refreshing:
yet they would not hear.

Isaiah 28:10-12

Notice "with stammering lips and another
tongue will he speak to this people.... This is the
rest...and refreshing...."

Speaking in tongues is a refreshing from the
cares of this world. When we allow the Holy Spirit
through our spirit to express Himself to God, it
does us more good than we can ever imagine!

A Sign for Unbelievers

Speaking in tongues is also a sign for the
unbeliever, as 1 Corinthians 14:21-22 says:

In the law it is written, With men of other
tongues and other lips will I speak unto this
people; and yet for all that will they not hear me,
saith the Lord. Wherefore tongues are for a sign,
not to them that believe, but to them that believe

not: but prophesying serveth not for them that believe not, but for them which believe.

When you bring unsaved people to the church and they hear people speaking in tongues, they may be convinced it is of God and desire the supernatural presence of God in their own lives.

Holy Spirit Intercession

Praying in tongues, or praying in the Holy Spirit, keeps us praying in line with the Word of God, especially in situations in which we don't know how or what to pray. Romans 8:26-28 says:

Likewise the Spirit also helpeth our infirmities [weaknesses]: for we know not what we should pray for as we ought: but the Spirit itself maketh intercession for us with groanings which cannot be uttered [put into regular words]. And he that searcheth the hearts knoweth what is the mind of the Spirit, because he maketh intercession for the saints according to the will of God. And we know that all things work together for good to them that love God, to them who are the called according to his purpose.

If we have a specific need and we know what God's Word says in that area, we need to pray according to His Word. As we do, we will be amazed at how things will work out. However, in situations in which we don't know how to pray as we should, we can simply say, "Lord, I don't know how to pray about this particular situation, so I will pray in the Holy Spirit and trust You that this situation will be addressed and resolved."

There is great reassurance in knowing we can pray in the Holy Spirit about everything. In fact, if we never spend time praying in tongues but do all our praying in English, then we are not fulfilling what Jesus said in John 4:23:

> But the hour cometh, and now is, when the true worshippers shall worship the Father in spirit and in truth: for the Father seeketh such to worship him.

When we speak in tongues, we worship the Father in spirit and in truth.

Spirit Communication

Another benefit of speaking in tongues is that it is the language with which the human spirit can communicate directly with God.

> For he that speaketh in an unknown tongue speaketh not unto men, but unto God: for no man understandeth him; howbeit in the spirit he speaketh mysteries.
>
> 1 Corinthians 14:2

Speaking in tongues allows us to speak mysteries or, literally in the Greek, *divine secrets* to God. We are not speaking to humans; we are speaking directly to God, discussing divine secrets.

Submitting the Tongue to God

Another benefit of speaking in tongues is that it causes the tongue to submit to God.

> But the tongue can no man tame; it is an unruly evil, full of deadly poison.
>
> James 3:8

James says that no man can tame the tongue; "it is an unruly evil." However, the Holy Spirit can tame the tongue and keep it under submission when we speak in tongues. The more time we spend speaking in tongues, the less time we have for our mouths to say things that cause trouble. Then we become more conscious of our speech and our obedience to God.

It Is Worth Doing!

We have seen from the Word of God that speaking in tongues every day is worth doing. It is beneficial and valuable. Take time every day to speak in tongues and become more acquainted with the Holy Spirit. Your spiritual life will become richer when you do!

4

Holy Spirit Manifestations

The face of God represents His glory, and in the Old Testament that glory was deadly. In Exodus when Moses asked to see God's face, for example, God told him he could not (Ex. 33:23). However, Jesus Christ made it possible for us to behold God's face—His glory—by supernatural acts of the Holy Spirit being manifested in the natural realm.

Second Corinthians 4:6 says that God's glory is revealed in Jesus:

> For God, who commanded the light to shine out of darkness, hath shined in our

hearts, to give the light of the knowledge of the glory of God in the face of Jesus Christ.

Second Corinthians 3:18 says, "We all, with open face beholding as in a glass the glory of the Lord...." To witness this glory, however, we must forsake tradition. When we become fervent in Spirit and pure in heart, we will see the greatest moves and manifestations of God ever witnessed on earth, as Haggai foretold:

> The glory of this latter house shall be greater than of the former, saith the Lord of hosts: and in this place will I give peace, saith the Lord of hosts.
>
> Haggai 2:9

The Bible is full of God's brilliance. When we believe and obey the Word, we see His glory manifest in our lives.

Acts 2:15 refers to one example of God's glory manifesting. Explaining the events of the Day of Pentecost, Peter says, "For these are not drunken, as ye suppose, seeing it is but the third hour of the day." A drunk person has trouble walking or even standing, and the potency of the infilling Holy Spirit can cause the same response.

There are numerous ways in the Scriptures that people respond to the manifestations of God's presence. One time, for example, a person's voice was affected by the Spirit of God. In the following Scriptures from Luke's gospel we read about this event:

> And Zacharias said unto the angel, Whereby shall I know this? for I am an old man, and my wife well stricken in years. And the angel answering said unto him, I am Gabriel, that stand in the presence of God; and am sent to speak unto thee, and to shew thee these glad tidings. And, behold, thou shalt be dumb, and not able to speak, until the day that these things shall be performed, because thou believest not my words, which shall be fulfilled in their season.
>
> Luke 1:18-20

> And he asked for a writing table, and wrote, saying, His name is John. And they marvelled all. And his mouth was opened immediately,

and his tongue loosed, and he spake, and praised God.

Luke 1:63,64

This story illustrates that the natural, human function of talking can be suspended by the presence of God. When the natural comes in contact with the supernatural, the supernatural will always prevail.

Another example of this truth is found in Acts 9. Here, Saul, who later became Paul, was knocked down by the power of God.

> And Saul arose from the earth; and when his eyes were opened, he saw no man: but they led him by the hand, and brought him into Damascus.
>
> And he was three days without sight, and neither did eat nor drink.

Acts 9:8,9

Notice how Paul's encounter with the presence of God affected him. Paul heard Jesus' voice, was knocked down by His glory, saw a vision, stood up, and was unable to see. For three days and three nights he was blind. Jesus' presence affected Paul not only spiritually but physically.

Another example of God's presence affecting human flesh is found in John 18, which records the moment when Judas, the Pharisees, and others came to apprehend Jesus to crucify Him.

> Jesus therefore, knowing all things that should come upon him, went forth, and said unto them, Whom seek ye?
>
> They answered him, Jesus of Nazareth. Jesus saith unto them, I am he. And Judas also, which betrayed him, stood with them. As soon then as he had said unto them, I am he, they went backward, and fell to the ground.
>
> John 18:4-6

These people fell down under the power of God. Jesus didn't even lay hands on them, but they could not stand up in the presence of God. I am amazed that this band of men had the audacity to arrest Jesus after falling backward under the power of God when in His presence!

Jesus said, "He that hath seen me hath seen the Father" (John 14:9). In 2 Corinthians, we learned that we can see the glory of God by looking in the face of Jesus. We do that by looking in the Bible, and when we do, supernatural things can start affecting our natural condition.

Another example of the supernatural affecting the natural is found in Matthew. The following passage tells us of certain Roman guards at Christ's burial site who started shaking for fear of an angel and became as dead men:

> And, behold, there was a great earthquake: for the angel of the Lord descended from heaven, and came and rolled back the stone from the door, and sat upon it. His countenance was like lightning, and his raiment white as snow: and for fear of him the keepers did shake, and became as dead men.
>
> Matthew 28:2-4

This Scripture says that when the angel, representing the presence of God, manifested at the resurrection of Jesus, he rolled back a stone and sat upon it. The angel did not touch the men. He did not breathe on them. He did not shoot lightning out of his fingertips. However, when these guards, who were in a sinful state, found themselves in the presence of God, they shook and became as dead men. Dead men don't stand; they lie down. Dead men don't move; they are out cold—literally cold!

The Scriptures contain many stories of people falling down when in the presence of the Lord. Look, for example, at how God's presence affected Jesus' disciples:

> And after six days Jesus taketh Peter, James, and John his brother, and bringeth them up into an high mountain apart, and was transfigured before them: and his face did shine as the sun, and his raiment was white as the light. And, behold, there appeared unto them Moses and Elias talking with him. Then answered Peter, and said unto Jesus, Lord, it is good for us to be here: if thou wilt, let us make here three tabernacles; one for thee, and one for Moses, and one for Elias. While he yet spake,

behold, a bright cloud overshadowed them:
and behold a voice out of the cloud, which
said, This is my beloved Son, in whom I am
well pleased; hear ye him. And when the disciples heard it, they fell on their face, and were
sore afraid.

Matthew 17:1-6

When Peter, James, and John heard a voice
(God's voice) from a cloud, they fell on their
faces and were afraid. No indication is given that
these men fell down voluntarily; quite the oppo-
site is implied.

And Jesus came and touched them, and
said, Arise, and be not afraid.

Matthew 17:7

In Acts, Paul recounts his own *falling down*
incident:

At midday, O king, I saw in the way a light
from heaven, above the brightness of the sun,
shining round about me and them which jour-
neyed with me. And when we were all fallen to
the earth, I heard a voice speaking unto me,

and saying in the Hebrew tongue, Saul, Saul, why persecutest thou me? it is hard for thee to kick against the pricks. And I said, Who art thou, Lord? And he said, I am Jesus whom thou persecutest.

Acts 26:13-15

It was not just Paul who was knocked down by the power of God. Paul's entire company experienced the manifested presence of God.

When we are astonished by God's power, something about us will change. Our voice, our ability to stand up, our ability to stay balanced, our vision, or our bodily functions may change. These changes demonstrate our flesh being totally overwhelmed by God's power.

It is exciting to see people fall under the power of God, but wait until you witness God popping them up from the floor!

As the appearance of the bow that is in the cloud in the day of rain, so was the appearance of the brightness round about. This was the appearance of the likeness of the glory of the

Lord. And when I saw it, I fell upon my face,
and I heard a voice of one that spake.

Ezekiel 1:28

And he said unto me, Son of man, stand
upon thy feet, and I will speak unto thee. And
the spirit entered into me when he spake unto
me, and set me upon my feet, that I heard him
that spake unto me.

Ezekiel 2:1,2

Ezekiel had a supernatural vision and fell
upon his face when he saw the glory of God—
and he did not get up on his own. There is more
in the Bible than we think!

The Bible even tells us about transportation
by the Spirit of God. Philip had a great mass
crusade beginning in Samaria, yet God knew
there was one individual in another location
who needed Philip. Philip had won practically
an entire city to the Lord, but after his return to
Jerusalem to continue preaching an angel spoke
to him and told him to go south.

Philip was obedient and joined himself to the Ethiopian eunuch's chariot. When he heard the man reading Isaiah, Philip ran over and asked if he understood what he was reading. When the man said, "How can I, except some man should guide me?" (Acts 8:31), Philip began from the point where the man was reading and preached Christ to him. The man was saved and baptized in water. Now notice what happens next in this chapter:

> And when they were come up out of the water, the Spirit of the Lord caught away Philip, that the eunuch saw him no more: and he went on his way rejoicing. But Philip was found at Azotus: and passing through he preached in all the cities, till he came to Caesarea.
>
> Acts 8:39,40

Philip was found in Azotus. In verse 39 *caught* is the same word used in 1 Thessalonians 4:17 in reference to the Rapture. The Holy Spirit supernaturally moved Philip from one city to another. Imagine what would happen in our churches if we saw a believer suddenly appear among us by supernatural transportation!

Now imagine what would happen if a believer seemed to be hit with an electrical bolt, get knocked backward fourteen feet, roll under a pew, then get lifted up in midair before being sat back to their original position by the Spirit and power of God. (Acts 9:3-4; 8:39; Ezek. 2:2.) In these biblical references it was not electricity. It was the Holy Spirit!

Second Chronicles 5:13-14 speaks of God's manifested presence affecting worshipers in a corporate setting:

> It came even to pass, as the trumpeters and singers were as one, to make one sound to be heard in praising and thanking the Lord; and when they lifted up their voice with the trumpets and cymbals and instruments of musick, and praised the Lord, saying, For he is good; for his mercy endureth for ever: that then the house was filled with a cloud, even the house of the Lord; so that the priests could not stand

to minister by reason of the cloud: for the glory
of the Lord had filled the house of God.

These priests could not stand because of the
glory of God that filled the house.

> Now when Solomon had made an end of
> praying, the fire came down from heaven, and
> consumed the burnt offering and the sacrifices;
> and the glory of the Lord filled the house. And
> the priests could not enter into the house of
> the Lord, because the glory of the Lord had
> filled the Lord's house.
>
> 2 Chronicles 7:1,2

So much glory of God was in the house of
the Lord that the priests could not even enter it!
The manifestation of God's power was such that
the priests could not walk through the door.
This cloud was so thick that there was no room
for human beings. The next verse tells of the
people's response.

> And when all the children of Israel saw how
> the fire came down, and the glory of the Lord
> upon the house, they bowed themselves with

their faces to the ground upon the pavement, and worshipped, and praised the Lord, saying, For he is good; for his mercy endureth for ever.

2 Chronicles 7:3

Similarly, in Acts 10, the Holy Spirit affected Peter's natural condition, and the results of his encounter with the Holy Spirit made a great impact on the kingdom of God:

On the morrow, as they went on their journey, and drew nigh unto the city, Peter went up upon the housetop to pray about the sixth hour: and he became very hungry, and would have eaten: but while they made ready, he fell into a trance.

Acts 10:9,10

This vision from Peter's trance led to the first Holy Spirit baptism of the Gentiles in his time. The Bible says the Spirit of God is like the wind. You cannot see which way the wind is going, but you can see the results of where it has been.

We have more than enough Scripture to evince differing and unusual manifestations of

God's Spirit among us today. As we wait on the Lord's return, we shall see more of God's Spirit manifested in ways that will seem strange, unusual, and extraordinary.

We can keep the supernatural flowing by staying in faith and fervent in Spirit. We cannot afford to get too religious or dignified. I don't think Saul was considered "dignified" as he lay there flat on his face on the Damascus road in front of his companions who were arresting Christians. It was this very same man who went on to write two-thirds of the New Testament. He had visions, trances, angelic visitations; even Jesus appeared to him supernaturally.

The more we reach for the heavenly throne, the more that throne takes up residency in our hearts and in our midst. The more the glory of God is manifested, the more people will be filled with His Spirit—which always begins with speaking in tongues.

5

How To Be Filled With the Spirit

If you would like to pray to be filled with the Holy Spirit with the evidence of speaking in tongues, I want to invite you to do so today. You don't have to ask God to send the Holy Spirit, because He is here. He has been with us since the Day of Pentecost. All you have to do is *receive Him.* You receive Him just as you received salvation—by a simple prayer of faith.[3]

Often people say that someone "got saved last night." No, that person became saved two

---

[3] If you have not already received salvation, I encourage you to turn to "Prayer of Salvation" at the end of this book before proceeding with the following prayer for the baptism in the Holy Spirit.

thousand years ago but *received* salvation last night. The same thing is true with the Holy Spirit. God sent Him two thousand years ago, along with your salvation. All you have to do is receive Him.

Some people imagine that the Holy Spirit is going to make them lose control. They think He will grab their tongue and make them say something, but He will not do that. In fact, if you wait for Him to do that, you will not receive.

Acts 2:4 shows us the Bible method of receiving the Holy Spirit:

> And they were all filled with the Holy Ghost, and began to speak with other tongues, *as the Spirit gave them utterance.*

When you are full of the Holy Spirit, you will begin to speak. The Word does not say that they were filled with the Holy Spirit and the Holy Spirit talked for them. Rather, it says that they were filled with the Holy Spirit and they began to speak. This means they opened their mouths and said something.

Notice that "the Spirit gave them utterance." The Holy Spirit gives the words, but we do the talking. When you keep repeating, "Father, I want to receive the Holy Spirit. Thank You, Jesus; thank You, Jesus..." or "Father, I want to receive the Holy Spirit," and then clam up frozen in fear, you are not in a position to receive. The Holy Spirit is a gentleman, and He won't just take over. You have to receive Him. If you close your mouth or keep talking in English, you will not receive. You have to open your mouth to speak.

If you desire to be filled with the Holy Spirit, pray this prayer:

Father, I thank You for the depth of You that is available to me. I ask You to baptize me now in your Holy Spirit. I pray for the initial evidence of the baptism of the Holy Spirit, the gift of tongues, which leads to the other eight gifts of Your Holy Spirit. Baptize me now. Lead and minister to me in the days ahead as never before. I yield myself to You and to Your ministry of supernatural workings. Father, I commit to keep my eyes upon You. In Jesus' name I pray. Amen.

Now just begin to speak, not in English but in the spirit. The Holy Spirit will guide you and give you the utterance. You receive this experience by faith, just as you received salvation. By faith you open your mouth and trust God to give you the utterance. God's Spirit gives the language as He fills you. Simply yield to Him, receive Him, and let those words come out from your belly. Out of your belly will flow rivers of living water. They will come up from your spirit, flow right over your vocal cords, and you will speak in other tongues.

Prayer of Salvation

God loves you—no matter who you are, no matter what your past. God loves you so much that He gave His one and only begotten Son for you. The Bible tells us that "...whoever believes in him shall not perish but have eternal life" (John 3:16 NIV). Jesus laid down His life and rose again so that we could spend eternity with Him in heaven and experience His absolute best on earth. If you would like to receive Jesus into your life, say the following prayer out loud and mean it from your heart.

Heavenly Father, I come to You admitting that I am a sinner. Right now, I choose to turn away from sin, and I ask You to cleanse me of all unrighteousness. I believe that Your Son, Jesus, died on the cross to take away my sins. I also believe that He rose again from the dead so that I might be forgiven of my sins and made righteous through faith in Him. I call upon the name of Jesus Christ to be the Savior and Lord of my life. Jesus, I choose to follow You and ask that You fill me with the power of the Holy Spirit. I declare that right now I am a child of God. I am free from sin and full of the righteousness of God. I am saved in Jesus' name. Amen.

If you prayed this prayer to receive Jesus Christ as your Savior for the first time, please contact us on the Web at **www.harrisonhouse.com** to receive a free book.

Or you may write to us at
Harrison House
P.O. Box 35035
Tulsa, Oklahoma 74153

About the Author

Best known for his bold teaching ministry based on the uncompromised full gospel, Pastor David Pizzimenti has made Hebrews 13:8 the foundational Scripture of his ministry: "Jesus Christ the same yesterday, and today, and for ever." God has used Pastor Pizzimenti extensively to minister the infilling of the Holy Spirit to the believer.

Pastor Pizzimenti is the founding pastor of Glory To Him Fellowship—a rapidly growing interdenominational and interracial church. Since its establishment on April 12, 1987, it has become one of the fastest growing full gospel churches in southern Alabama.

Pastor Pizzimenti is a 1977 graduate of Kenneth E. Hagin's Rhema Bible Training Center. From 1990 until 1997, David served as a minister to ministers as district director of Alabama for Rhema Ministerial Association, International. Currently he serves as a member of the board of directors of Jesse Duplantis Ministries.

Pastor Pizzimenti is a strong supporter and promoter of Israel and the Bible lands. Since 1987 he has led more than twenty tours to the Holy Land and has met with the prime minister of Israel and other leading government officials.

Pastor Pizzimenti accepts ministry engagements across the United States and abroad.
To schedule a meeting or receive a complete book and teaching tape catalog, please write to:

David Pizzimenti Ministries
P.O. Box 1289
Ozark, Alabama 36361
or e-mail us at
gthf@charter.net

You may learn more about
David Pizzimenti Ministries
by visiting our Web site:
www.dpministries.org

*Please include your prayer requests
and comments when you write.*

If this book has been a blessing to you
or if you would like to see more of the
Harrison House product line,
please visit us on our Web site at
www.harrisonhouse.com.

HARRISON HOUSE
Tulsa, Oklahoma 74153

The Harrison House Vision

Proclaiming the truth and the power
Of the Gospel of Jesus Christ
With excellence;

Challenging Christians to
Live victoriously,
Grow spiritually,
Know God intimately.